ALL LEON
and Province

Text: Rosa Mª Sánchez.
Photographs: Luis Miguel Ramos Blanco / FISA-Escudo de Oro.

Special thanks to Don José Antonio Reyero for his photographic collaboration.

Our most sincere thanks to all the institutions who provided all that necessary in the production of this book, and a special thanks to the Leon Museum (Autonomous Government of Castilla and Leon), to the Cathedral and its Museum, to the San Marcos Hostel and to the Saint Isidoro Basilica.

Design, lay-out and printing, entirely created by the technical department of EDITORIAL ESCUDO DE ORO, S.A.

Copyright of this edition for photographs and text:
© EDITORIAL ESCUDO DE ORO, S.A.
Palaudàries, 26 - 08004 Barcelona (Spain).

e-mail: editorial@eoro.com
http://www.eoro.com

Editorial Escudo de Oro, S.A.

View of a snow covered Leon.

THE BIMELLINNEIAL CITY OF LEON

Situated on level ground at the confluence of the Torío and Bernesga rivers, the city of Leon is located 822 metres above sea level, and there is record of its existence as a city since the year 74 of the Christian Era when the VII Gémina Legion established itself where some clearly military archaeological remains from earlier times were found. According to all indications a detachment, presumably the VI Legion, was already established in the city around the years 10 and 15 before Christ, as in 1998 a mud wall was found together with a second wall and some large military huts which date back to just a few years after this time, under the rule of Augustus or Tiberius.

From this strategic position control of the large gold mines in Las Medulas and Bierzo was intented, as well as guarding and defending the recently conquered zones in the north. Thanks to the two memorial tablets found in the Villalís de la Valduerna locality which date back to the years 163 and 184, the exact date of the foundation of the VII Legion can be known: 10 June in the year 68 of the Christian Era.

The VII Legion had a rectangular encampment which measured approximately 20 hectares, the longer side measuring 570 metres and the shorter side 350 metres. Apart from the legionaries, a surrounding settlement was also established giving rise to the city of Leon whose name is a derivation of Legio.

The boundaries of the old Roman settlement were used as the limits of the medieval enclosure. The present wall, which should not be confused with the medieval wall close by, still preserves the original Romanesque structure, except for some later restorations and additions.

From the end of the 3rd century there is no recorded documentation of the city until 585 when it fell under the power of Leovigildo and was integrated into the Visigoth dominion, confirming earlier minting during the Suintila era (621-631).

Under the hand of the Berber Tariq ibn Ziyad the Muslims invaded Leon around 712, and two years later Musa ibn Nusayr began his campaign against Lugo from the capital. Until Alfonso I the Catholic reconquered a large part of the North Meseta the city did not free itself from Muslim domain. The full integration of the Leonese capital into the Asturian kingdom took place around the mid 9th century when Ordoño II conquered the city finally, and in this way began the Leonese medieval history.

Leon's historical protagonism began when Alfonso II died and his heir, García, moved the Asturian kingdom's capital to the Leonese capital. Around the times of Vermudo II the head of state, Almanzor, stormed, looted, and set the city alight after a four day resistance. Alfonso VI the Nobleman reconstructed and repopulated the city, reinforcing its walls, and in August 1017 the first territorial laws of the Spanish Middle Age were proclaimed, usually

Partial view of the Leonese walls.

Stamp of privilege by Pedro I, Cathedral Museum.

Roman bridge and the San Marcos Inn.

Mercado or Grano Square.

called the *Fuero* of Leon. Some years later Fernando I and his wife, *doña* Sancha, rebuilt the San Juan Bautista church as a royal pantheon, and in 1063 they had Saint Isidore's remains brought from Seville.

The Leonese Empire became established, although not very strongly, under Alfonso VII, crowned «Imperator» in the cathedral of Leon in 1135 with the help of his Vassals from Navarra, Barcelona, and Tolosa. Subsequently, in 1188 Alfonso IX convoked a Regal Curia and for the first time the city's representatives assisted –the bourgeois– and this gave rise to the first democratic courts in Europe.

After the re-conquest the course of the *Tagus* river weakened the influence of Leon, and in 1230 it lost its reign as a capital over this area which became part of the Castilla kingdom. In spite of this, during the 13th and 14th centuries the city converted itself in an important Castillian trading centre, and towards the south an important area for the seasonal migration of cattle. In 1348 the Black Death worsened the demographic deficit, and apart from the recuperation of 1751 on account of the first grand linen factory (ruined in 1769) the city was at a standstill until the early 19th century. At this time the great urban expansion began and the city expanded to outside the walls. Then in the 20th century it expanded to such a degree that it became one of the most important capital cities of Spain. Although it still does suffer a shortage of important industrial trade the city orientates itself around the services sector, and its economic influence resides in its capacity to generate richness from mining and agriculture.

Aerial view of Leon with the cathedral in the forefront.

Night view of the Cathedralic temple. ▷

THE CATHEDRAL

This is one of the most beautiful examples of ogival art. It rises out of the same plot of land which was home to the Roman hot springs and the old Roman cathedral which was demolished in order to build the present one. The cathedral was constructed in the 13th century under the direction of Enrique of Burgos who overlooked the works until 1277, and under Juan Pérez until 1296. The ground plan consists of three naves, and its construction is quite similar to that of the Reims cathedral in France. Gregorio Marañón said that the temple resembles «a petrified ship which, on crossing the Pajares port and contemplating the Castilla la Vieja plains –from there it seems like a sea with scarcely a wave– it emerges un-expectedly in the middle of the meseta, where the hills which outline the horizon are not mountains created by God but castles and cathedrals made by man».

Although it is fundamentally a building from the 13th century the construction of this cathedral in Leon continued in later centuries, and especially during the 14th century. The clock tower was built in the 15th century, and during the 16th century a part of the main gable end. A special mention must be given to the restorations which took place because of the feebleness of the foundations and the bad quality of the construction materials used. In 1631 the central vault of the transept was demolished and a vast baroque cupola was built. Later, as a precautionary measure against unexpected collapse Joaquín Churriguera positioned four pinnacles over the corresponding

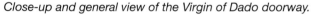

Close-up and general view of the Virgin of Dado doorway.

Doorway dedicated to Saint Froilán, South façade. ▷

transept pillars. In spite of everything, around the mid 19th century this part of the temple had such a ruinous aspect that the architect Matías Laviña proceeded to get rid of Churriguera's additions. Towards the end of the 19th century Juan Madrazo, Demetrio de los Ríos and Juan Bautista Lázaro carried out a profound restoration on the temple which affected the vaults, transepts, and the stained glass windows. Architecturally speaking, on the exterior of the temple the north-facing façade is the façade which has been preserved the most, and at the same time that which has been most affected by meteorological conditions. Its main doorway is from the 13th century and the only one which conserves the original polychroming from the 15th century because of the fact that it is protected by the walls of the cloister. The Virgin of Dado presides the scene, and in the

tympanum there is a representation of the Pantocrator surrounded by the four evangelists or Tetramerous. The jambs are adorned with the figures of Saint Paul, Saint Peter, James, the Visitation, and the evangelist Saint Matthew.

The south façade which was totally repaired in the 19th century and is located opposite the bishop's palace, has three doorways. The central doorway is dedicated to Saint Froilán, the bishop of Leon and patron saint of the Leonese diocese whose effigy presides the axis. The tympanum displays the Pantocrator and the four evangelists in a posture of writing on their respective pulpits. The jambs are decorated with the images of the Annunciation, the prophet Samuel, and the Three Kings.

On the doorway on the right there are scenes of the removal of Saint Froilán's remains from the monas-

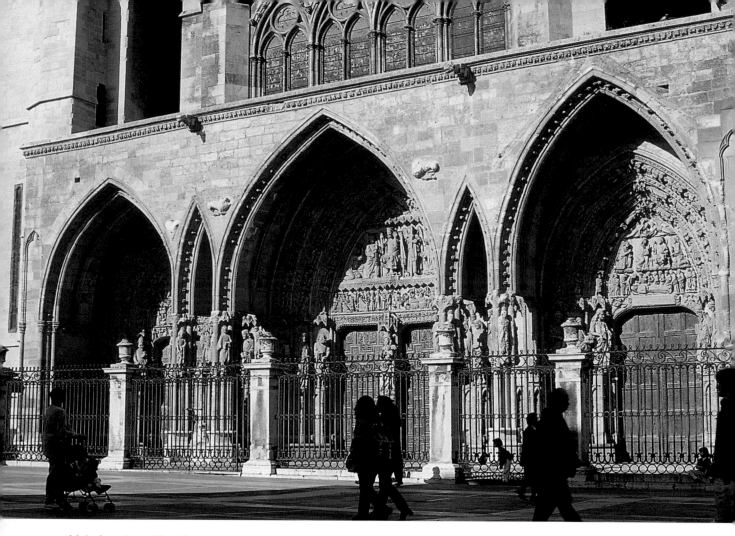

Main façade or West façade.

tery in Moreruela to the Cathedral. Finally, the doorway on the left called the Death doorway displays heraldic motifs of lions and castles which decorate the jambs, lintels and archivolts.

The main west-facing façade is enriched with a beautiful portico which has three arcades. The sculptures are of extraordinary artistic quality, and especially the copy of the marvellous image of the White Virgin, a work from the mid-13th century whose author is anonymous, and whose original can be admired in the central chapel of the nave surrounding the apse. The lintel of the door displays floral motifs and a frieze depicting a scene from the Last Supper which includes Saint Michael in the centre weighing the souls, the seated figure of Christ, two angels, the Virgin, and Saint John.

The doorway on the left is dedicated to Saint John, and displays a series of bands on the tympanum which depict scenes of the life of Jesus and His Mother. On the jambs there are representations of Solomon, David, Saint John, Saint Peter, and the Judgement, a legend in gothic characters which states «Justice is in giving each person what is rightly his». A small marble column on this façade brings to mind the «locus apellationis», a place where the juridical committee of Leon used to congregate in order to settle conflicts.

The Saint Francis door is located to the right of the west façade, and its tympanum depicts scenes of the sleeping and crowning of the Virgin. The archivolts are adorned with angels, archangels, and an allusive scene of the foolish and prudent virgins. The jambs exhibit figures of the Queen of Sheba, the sibyl of Eritrea, Isaiah, Simon, Saint John, and Jesus.

Main façade: copy of the beautiful White Virgin and sculptures of Saint John, Santiago el Mayor, and Saint Peter.

Tympanum and frieze of the Last Supper: the grand theatre of the end of time. Christ His Majesty contemplating the infinity.

Tympanum and frieze of the Saint John Doorway.

Sculptures on one of the jambs of the Saint John Doorway, and the «locus apellationis» where political and legal judgements were carried out.

Sculptures on the jambs of the Saint Francis Doorway.

Tympanum and frieze of the Saint Francis Doorway depicting the death, removal, and crowning of the Virgin.

Windows in the transept and the upper part.

One of the most beautiful parts of this cathedral must be the stained glass windows which depict all the epochs from the 13th century through to the 19th century. The inside of the temple is amazingly enriched by this collection of representations in glass which filter the light and grant a unreal ambience. The decoration includes themes from the life of man and the history of the Christian salvation. In the lower part the plant life alternates with the arts, the sciences, the virtues, and the vices. The heraldic shields are reserved for the triforium, and in the upper part images of saints, prophets, monarchs, and other important personages are depicted in the large windows. A total of thirty-one windows of great dimensions, se-

Rose windows on the west side: a miracle of colour and transparency.

North rose window.

venty-four triforium windows, ten in the lower part, three large rose windows, and the stained glass windows in the Virgin of the Road chapel sums a total of one thousand eight hundred square metres of glass. In all probability the first skilled workmen who worked on the stained glass windows were French, some of whom were brought from the cathedral in Burgos. From this stage there are various panels, like the rose windows on the north side and the first stained glass window on the south side. An exceptional and impressive stained glass window called the «*Cacería*» (the hunt) has also been preserved, and some experts say

High windows located on the north side of the main nave (14th century).

Silver urn holding Saint Froilán's remains.

that it originally came from the palace of *doña* Beren-guela because of the scenes it depicts, a mixture of scenes of circuses, minstrels, and mounted horsemen. The complex restoration suffered by the cathedral in the late 19th century generated a thorough inspection of the artistic works not pertaining to the style of the temple in the Main Chapel. Because of this, the baroque reredos was dismounted and replaced by a collection of early paintings, work of Nicolás Francés. It originally consisted of eighteen panels and more than three hundred smaller international gothic panels. The present work narrates scenes from the lives of Saint Froilán and the Virgin, and other works from the late 15th century by an artist known as the master of Palanquin. An image of the Assumption, patroness of the cathedral, from the 18th century occupies an important position over the Bishop's throne.

At the beginning of the 20th century the Leonese silversmiths, Neira and Candanedo, made a silver urn which can be found under the main altar, and contains Saint Froilán's remains.

In the upper wings two sepulchres, on the right and left, reminds us of the burials of Saint Alvito and Saint Pelayo. And finally, on the right, the Door of Thistle carved by Juan de Badajoz el Viejo (the Old Man) around 1515 resolves itself into an authentic filigree of stone in Hispanic-Flemish style.

The only royal burial in the cathedral, that of Ordoño II, is to be found in the area behind the altar. Traditionally, this king was awarded the honour of having donated his palace for the construction of the original temple. The figure of the reclining king, and the scenes of the death of Christ are from the 13th century. The remaining funeral scenes are from the 15th century.

Tomb of King Ordoño II located behind the altar.

Some of the cathedral's chapels contain some very interesting artistic pieces, like the sepulchre of Bishop don Rodrigo in the Virgin of Carmelite chapel. The Santo Cristo chapel displays an extraordinary reredos of Juan de Valmaseda from the 16th century, and the Virgin of the Road by Juan de Badajoz el Viejo in 1504 is a late Gothic masterpiece.

The retrochoir, work of Juan de Badajoz el Mozo (the Boy) began in the early 16th century but was not terminated until 1585. It is done in a triumphal arch style and the beautiful alabaster medallions are the work of Stephen Jordan.

Juan de Valmaseda reredos in the Santo Cristo chapel, and the Virgen del Camino chapel.

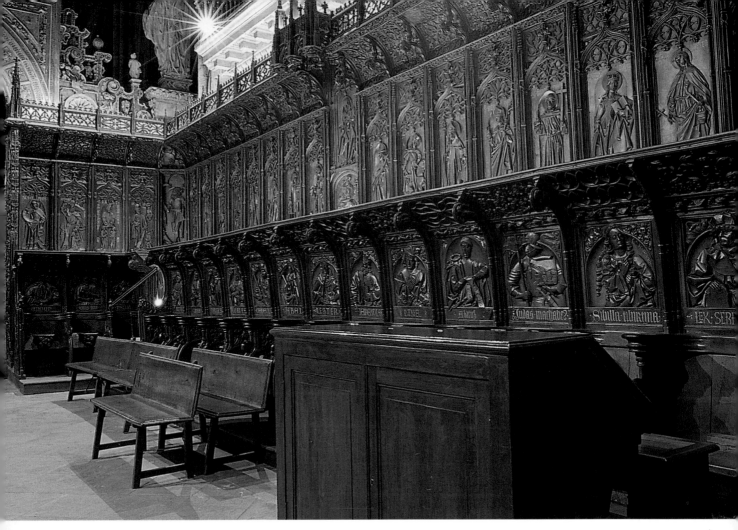

Cathedralic choir stalls.

One aspect of the cloister gallery. ▷

This Leonese cathedral's choir is an exceptional flaming Gothic work carved in walnut by Central European artists like Juan de Malinas and Copin from Holland in the second half of the 15th century. The choir stalls are divided into two parts, the King's choir and the Bishop's choir, and both are beautifully and artistically carved.

Around the 17th century the cathedral's cloister underwent a total reformation. The original roofing from the 13th and 14th centuries was changed under the supervision of Juan de Badajoz el Mozo. The four fronts of the wall with its arches and capitals are also from this epoch while the vaults and pillars are from the Renaissance era. Since the 13th century the cloister has been used for the various burials of Leonese aristocrats: Gothic sepulchres of the dean Martín Fernández and Domingo Juan in the

west wing and in the south wall, and under the Romanesque relief of the Virgin of the Forum and Offerings, which recalls the annual Leonese City Council offering, is the tomb of Munio Ponzardi.

The cloister's frescos date back to the 15th century and are the work of Nicolás Francés, but because of the rough weather co17r the years they have begun to disappear. The last restoration which took place in 1994 succeeded in returning the scenes of the life of Christ to their original splendour in spite of the damage caused by the harsh weather.

All the cloister's vaults, and especially the tiercelon vaults, were adorned with silver motifs by Juan de Badajoz el Mozo in the 16th century. The combination of all these elements make this cloister one of the most magnificent of the Spanish Renaissance era.

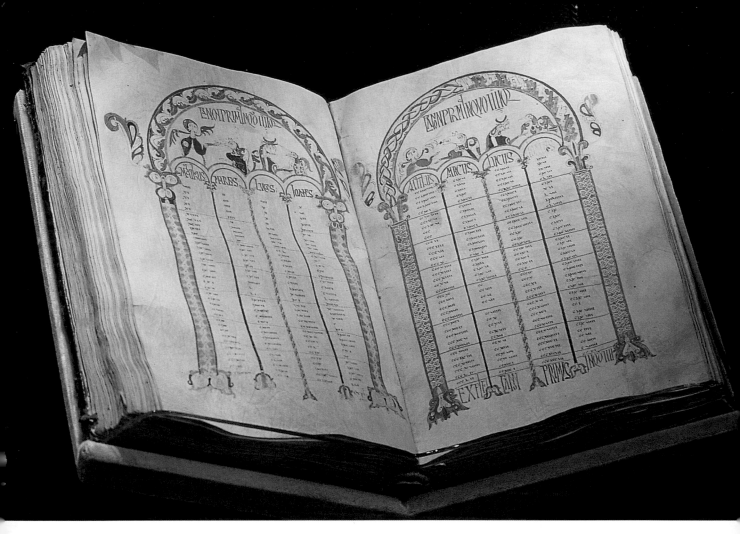

Mozarabic bible from the 10th century.

DIOCESAN CATHEDRALIC MUSEUM

In 1981 the Cathedral's Museum was merged with the Diocesan Museum which was located in the Seminary. The exceptional collection of religious, documentary, and archaeological art which forms a part of this rich heritage make this museum one of the most important in Spain. The reform which took place in 1998 shows its vitality and capacity to adapt to these modern times, as various new halls dedicated to religious works by contemporary artists were inaugurated.

The Mozarabic bible from 920 adorned with abundant miniatures and written by Juan Diácono must be pointed out. The Visigothic antiphony from the 10th century is also one of the Museum's jewels. The music it contains, and which originates from the Hispanic liturgy, has not as yet been deciphered. The Book of Writings or the Testaments of the Kings of Leon, with portraits of monarchs and records of their donations to the cathedral, dates back to the 12th century.

The collections of images of the Virgin and Child originally come from the old Diocesan Museum, and pertain to the transitional period between the Roman and Gothic eras. The majority of these images originate in the various villages of the diocese, although they were brought together to protect them from disappearance and deterioration, and they reflect the artistic richness of this province's churches.

Various paintings by Nicolás Francés, some of which were found in the sides of the cathedral's Main altar and Bishop's throne, have recently been added to the Museum's heritage. In the same way the coffer containing the remains of Saint Froilán work of Juan de Arfe around 1520, is now on exhibition in the Halls of Treasures.

Juan de Juni crucifix.

The archaeological pieces from the prehistoric and Roman times are of exceptional interest, and the stone room is dedicated to various remains –some of which come from the old Romanesque cathedral– together with the Gothic sculptures of Ordoño II and the archangel Gabriel which are of great artistic quality and interest.

An extraordinarily dramatic crucifix by Juan de Juni, ivory sculptures, paintings signed by Pedro de Campaña and Salvador Maella, or sculptures by Berruguete, Gaspar Becerra, Gregorio Fernández, Salvador Carmona, or Pietro Torrigiano are all on display in the various halls in this museum. Furthermore, the visitor is also offered the opportunity to admire a unique collection of fabrics which begin in the 15th century and go right through to the 20th century, and there is an area dedicated to Coptic fabrics dating from the 14th to the 17th centuries.

Hall of fabrics.

Main façade of the Saint Isidore Basilica.

SAINT ISIDORE BASILICA

This is one of the most important and most beautiful Romanesque ensembles in Spain. It is a truly magnificent monument combining various arts which give an idea of the splendid past of the Leon Kingdom during the medieval epoch.

The Royal Basilica of Saint Isidore occupies the same site as the simple monastery dedicated to Saint Pelayo which was built, under the order of Sancho el Craso (the Coarse), in 966. Adjacent to this there was a monastery dedicated to Saint John the Baptist, and, like the aforementioned, it was demolished during the times of Almanzor towards the end of the 10th century. Alfonso V carried out a modest reconstruction, and later, Fernando I and his wife *doña* Sancha chose this site as a royal burial grounds. In 1603 Saint Isidore's

remains were brought from Seville, and the new church to which a new square-shaped west portico was added was inaugurated at the end of this same year. This new portico, whose ceilings were decorated in tempera, was chosen as the Royal Pantheon.

The present church was constructed towards the end of the 11th century thanks to the interest taken by *doña* Urraca in enlarging the spot where her parents' remains rested. Pedro Deustamben was in charge of this extension which culminated in a new consecration in 1149.

The temple displays a Latin cross ground plan and it is formed by three aisles with three apses in the most pure Romanesque style. Around the beginning of the 16th century the main chapel was demolished and substituted by the present decadent Gothic chapel. The temple also includes two beautiful doorways on the south side called the Cordero (Lamb) and the Perdón (Pardon).

The main doorway of this temple is popularly known as the Cordero, and Isaac's sacrifice is depicted on the tympanum. Saint Isidore and Saint Pelayo are effigiated in the two sculptures to be found on either side of the doorway, and the zodiac situated on the upper part as well as the remaining figures are considered to be from the original construction. Saint Isidore on horseback presides the balustrade and the pediment which are both baroque.

The fascinating Romanesque Perdón doorway is considered to be the work of the expert Esteban, and it is presided by the figures of Saint Peter and Saint Paul, together with reliefs which decorate the tympanum. The one on the right depicts the three Marys contemplating the empty tomb, in the centre a beautiful image of the Descent of Christ from the cross, and on the left the Ascension of Jesus while being unusually pushed by the apostles.

From the Quiñones chapel one can contemplate the north doorway with its beautiful marble columns, and whose capitals were decorated it seems, by the Master of the Serpents.

The central nave of the temple has a barrel vault, while the side aisles are arris, and the transept has evidence of Mauresque influences on the lobes of the arches. Since the 13th century the Quiñones

Cordero (Lamb) Doorway.

Perdón (Pardon) Doorway.

Saint Isidore Cloister, las Cabezadas.

Pantheon of the Kings. ▷

chapel has been decorated with exquisite mural paintings. For its part, in the Hispanic-Flemish Santo Martino chapel there is an urn which holds the remains of this saint.

The Saint Isidore Basilica also reckons with two cloisters, one from the beginning of the 16th century –which includes a Romanesque front from the 11th century– and another Baroque cloister from the 18th century.

PANTHEON OF THE KINGS

The Royal Pantheon which is set at the foot of the church on the west side of the building measures eight metres in length and is square-shaped. The ceiling exhibits a collection of Romanesque paintings, and in the centre it has three naves with two columns of great dimensions. The capitals are the first in the history of Spanish art which represent evangelical stories together with plant and floral decoration.

The paintings in the Royal Pantheon are considered to be pieces of art of unsurpassable quality; it is no wonder that this is called the «Sistine Chapel of Romanesque Art». The frescos depict some of the most important images from the New Testament, including a calendar of agricultural tasks, and Christ as the Pantocrator surrounded by the Tetramerous. There are eleven kings and thirteen queens, as well as various infantas, counts, and noblemen buried in this Pantheon. Among others, Alfonso V, Bermudo III, the infanta *doña* Sancha whose body has been preserved intact, and *don* García, the last count of Castilla.

Los Esmaltes arch from the 12th century.

SAINT ISIDORE MUSEUM

An ample hall, which can be accessed from the left side of the building and which has been equipped as a library specialising in religion, history, and art, serves as the vestibule to an enclosure which exhibits, among other things, a unique collection of medieval craftsmanship in precious metals in Spain.

But first we must mention the notable reservoir of Roman pieces, memorial tablets, and seals belonging to the VII Gémina Legion, and which were discovered by García and Bellido during the excavations on the lands adjacent to the Roman wall. Just like the very interesting tombstone which represents the Asturian Pintallus, who died in the Rhine, wearing a bearskin. The spiral staircase to the old palace rooms accedes to the area where the treasures of the Basilica are guarded, treasures which are now a pale reflec-

tion on what they were originally after suffering various robberies and looting which resulted in the disappearance of many objects. Some of the most important pieces are: Coffer of ivories with ivory plaques from 1059 where the relics of Saint John the Baptist and Saint Pelayo rest; a Scandinavian ivory box from the 10th century; an ivory peace plate with the Pantocrator from the 11th century; the Coffer of Relics made in 1063 which contained Saint Isidore's remains; *doña* Urraca's chalice formed of two pieces of onyx mounted in gold; the Coffer of enamel from the 13th century and a silver coffer made in the Middle East around the mid-11th century.

And finally, the Archive-Library displays its precious manuscripts and reservoir of documents, among which we should mention the Book of Job which dates back to 951 and a Mozarabic bible with exquisite miniatures from 960.

Marfiles arch (11th century).

Coffer of Relics (11th century).

The historical pennant of Baeza.

Doña Urraca chalice (11th century).

Main façade of the San Marcos Inn.

San Marcos Inn church. ▷

SAN MARCOS

It is one of the most spectacular of all the Spanish plateresque architecture. After various vicissitudes and uses, including the fact that it was used as a prison for Francisco de Quevedo, this building was cleaned up and restored and has become one of the most luxurious Tourist Inn's in Spain, as well as one of the best hotels in Europe.

Records of this place go back as far as the beginnings of peregrination when it was a hospital and inn. The Santiago Order took charge of its installations which were rebuilt, although around the beginning of the 16th century it was in danger of collapse. It was then that the major work began on the building which we see today and which served as the Order's emblematic building, as they celebrated their general chapters here.

The San Marcos façade displays an admirable archi-

tectural balance. Its construction began in 1533 and it was not terminated until 1541. The medallions, balconies, niches and crests alternate with extravagance through the whole ensemble, and there is also an imposing entrance, a tower on the left, and the church façade on the right. A motif which is constantly repeated is the shell of the pilgrims who passed by these walls on their way to Santiago. The medallions on the right represent various mythological, biblical, and historical characters. The majority of those on the right are portraits of the Santiago Order's teachers.

On the church's façade, on either side of the doorway, there are two niches with excellent embossing, especially that called the Descent, work of Juan de Juni. Until the reign of Carlos V work did not begin in the temple. The person responsible for this work is considered to be Juan de Orozco, during the time when construction was in effete Gothic. The arches

Chapter hall, one of the rooms, royal suite and flight of steps in the San Marcos Inn.

San Marcos choir.

Cloister and belfry. ▷

under the choir are indeed ogival, as are those which conform the church ceilings, much lower than the impressive main nave. The doorways with Renaissance traces, as well as the medallions and choir balustrades, demonstrate the vague style of the epoch.

The choir, elaborated in walnut, is a masterpiece among the Spanish choir stalls of the time. Three expertise workmen collaborated in its elaboration: Guillermo Doncel, Juan de Angers, and Juan de Juni, the latter being the inventor of the main idea and the originator of some of the most successful carvings and statues.

The cloister is the realisation of the stylistic ideas of Juan de Badajoz el Mozo. Having been built during two different epochs there is no evidence of the passing of time between the two interventions. As is

the norm in this artist's work, exuberance reigns in the decoration of the medallions in the vault's keystones, and in the adornments on the ledges of the arches. In the lower part there is a grand relief by Juan de Juni which depicts the Birth of Christ.

The cloister and some of the other rooms of the temple are occupied by the Museum of Leon. Some of these areas, as is the case of the Sacristy, are true jewels in plateresque architecture designed by Juan de Badajoz el Mozo.

The collection of tablets and inscriptions to be found in the cloister is considered to be the best in Spain, the majority of which is Romanesque and Vadiniense, towns related by marriage to Asturians and Cantabrians. The memorial tablet dedicated to Diana, the goddess of hunting, which seems to represent a warrior, is most impressive with its allusive texts and

Hall in the Archaeological Museum.

an idol, and it dates back to between 1,800 and 1,500 AD originating in Tabuyo del Monte.

The quantity and quality of artistic objects exhibited in the Museum of Leon make it extremely difficult to describe them all. We will therefore outline some of the most important. The memorial tablet with Greek inscriptions by Quintanilla de Somoza. The Christ by Carrizo de Ribera in ivory, carved in the 11th century. The cross of Peñalba donated by Ramiro II to the church of Santiago de Peñalba in Bierzo. The Calvary of Corullón, a locality close to Villafranca del Bierzo, from the 12th century. There are also various works from Juan de Juni, and an extraordinary head of Saint Francis which was carved by Luis Salvador Carmona in 1760.

Christ of Carrizo (11th century).

Sacristy. ▷

Guzmanes Palace.

GUZMANES PALACE

This is one of the most important civil architectural buildings in the city. It is currently occupied by the County Council.

The building was owned by the important Guzman family and designed by Rodrigo Gil de Hontañón who began work in 1559.

The main façade of the palace with its distinguished air is formed by a wall of great dimensions crowned by a gallery, and two turrets on the sides.

The lintel windows display artistic railings, and the Guzman coat of arms has been carved in many parts of the building.

The doorway is graceful and elegant, and it has the peculiarity of not being situated in the centre of the building but on the right.

The patio displays an architecture full of majestic grace: galleries of arches supported over ionic columns, and once again the Guzman coat of arms is repeated.

BOTINES BUILDING

This building designed by Antonio Gaudi as a textile warehouse and currently home to a financial body is to be found adjacent to the Guzman Palace. The surname of one of the associates, Botinás, was to determine the future name of the building. This building has an architecture which brings to mind the architecture used in the palaces built in medieval times, and without doubt, it is a visual jewel for the visitor.

THE OLD CITY COUNCIL

In 1998 the Municipal Corporation vacated this building designed by Juan de Ribero around the mid-16th century, and the City Council moved its headquarters to a modern building on Ordoño II street. The interior of the building contains stained glass windows designed by Luis García Zurdo and a mural by Vela Zanetti.

THE WALLS

In spite of the passing of the centuries, the Arabic invasion, and the expansion of the city, the nucleus of the Roman walls built during the late imperial epoch, towards the end of the 3rd century, have managed to arrive to the present day in relatively good condition. The enclosure corresponds to the original delimitation of the Roman encampment, and it had various gates

Botines Building.

Interior of the San Martin Church.

of which only one still survives today in the north of the city, the Castle Gate. The expansion of the medieval metropolis, and the destruction caused on the south side motivated Alfonso XI to enlarge the walled enclosure by means of a «fence» with a double wall and loopholes towards the end of the 14th century. Some of these walls can be contemplated from Cercas street, between the areas of the San Francisco garden and the Riaño square in the Húmedo district.

SANTA MARIA DEL MERCADO

This building is set in one of the most typical spots of the city. The church conserves part of its Romanesque structure from the 12th century, and the railings are also from this epoch. In the interior, one can worship the Piedad (Piety) from the 15th century, known as being dedicated to the Market or to the old Road (to Santiago).

SAN MARTIN CHURCH

The founding of this church dates back to the 11th century, but today nothing actually remains from the original structure. It was rebuilt in the 13th century, and the main chapel and the window invisible from the outside are from this era. In the interior of the building there is a beautiful sculpture of the Piedad, work of Luis Salvador Carmona, which was carefully restored after a fire.

SANTA MARINA CHURCH

This was the old temple of the Company of Jesus after having been founded in the 16th century, although it was abandoned when the Jesuits were expelled during the times of Carlos III. Later, in the 17th century it was extended. The ground-plan has the shape of a Latin

Virgin of the Rosary in the Santa Marina Church.

San Francisco Church.

cross and the vast nave is closed by a barrel vault decorated with geometrical motifs. In its interior it guards an extraordinary baroque organ which, even today, is to be found in perfect condition although it was fabricated in 1749 and originally came from the Santa María de Sandoval monastery. The image of the Virgin of the Rosary by Juan de Juni is one of the sculptural jewels of the church, as is the statue in alabaster of don Juan of San Millán, work of Stephen Jordan.

SAN FRANCISCO CHURCH

It shelters in its interior the main part of the baroque reredos which was originally in the Cathedral until its restoration in the 19th century. It consists of two side walls and a central main altar which depicts scenes of the life of the Virgin. It is the work of the Tomé brothers.

SAN MARCELO CHURCH

In medieval times this was a monastery and a hospital. The present building is from the 16th century, and on the inside rest the remains of the Roman centurion Marcelo, patron saint of the city and martyred in Tangiers. The sculpture of this saint is by Gregorio Fernández, also the author of the amazing Christ of Balderas which can be found in the chapel on the right, and the Immaculate which is in the chapel on the left.

PALAZ DEL REY CHURCH

Nothing remains of the outer part of this building which was ordered built by King Ramiro II as a palace, a church, and a pantheon. Excavations have revealed that the structure of this building was Mozarabic, which makes this the oldest church in Leon.

Palaz del Rey Church.

Main Square.

SAN JUAN AND SAN PEDRO DE RENUEVA

The main doorway from the 18th century which was adapted to this church originally came from the San Pedro de Eslonza monastery, abandoned and destroyed after the Deamortisation. It was designed by brother Pedro Martínez of Cerdeña in 1711. For the laterals, the corresponding entrances to the refectory and the chapter house of the monastery were also utilised.

MAIN SQUARE AND THE OLD CONSISTORY

The traditional market selling products from the neighbouring villages and towns still takes place in

Doorway of the Renueva Church.

this square. The main building in the square is the Old Consistory which was used since its construction in the 18th century for holding public events, like for example bullfighting.

STATELY HOMES

Leon reckons with a number of emblazoned mansions worth mentioning, like that on Serranos street which was built in the 17th century and belonged to the Marquis of Lorenzana. An older house is the palace which belonged to the Counts of Luna, with its 14th century façade and its turret from the 16th century. The house belonging to the alderman Hernando de Villafañe from the 17th century can be found opposite the City Council, and in the Torres de Omaña square one can admire the magnificent palace of Cardinal Lorenzana from the 18th century. The Carnicerías house is today an exhibitions hall and it was designed by Juan de Ribero in the 17th century.

Close-up of the doorway of the Count of Luna Palace.

Marquis of Villasinda Palace façade.

Inmaculada Square.

On Ancha street, close to the County Council, the important Leonese family, the Quiñones, had a palace built in the 17th century, and today it is known as the house of the Marquis of Villasinda, and on Fernández Cadórniga street a towered mansion from the 17th century displays the Osorio family shield.

The Hospital de Regla, situated beside the cathedral on the side street Arco de las Cien Doncellas, displays a striking baroque façade considered to be one of the most important in the city. It comes from Renedo de Valdetuéjar and belonged to the aristocratic Prado family. The Door of the Queen which is a setting for the Provincial Hearings on Cid street was originally a spinning mill built in Leon under the rule of Fernando VI, and whose effigy and that of his wife, Queen María, are to be seen on both of the medallions over the entrance arch.

THE CITY

The recent urban ordination plans for the suburban development (Polígono 10, Chantría and Eras de Renueva) have succeeded in making Leon a grand city, with its ample streets and finely designed squares flanked by modern buildings.

Many of the unique buildings were built around the first third of the 20th century during a time of extraordinary urban expansion. The Leonese architect Manuel de Cárdenas is responsible for two buildings which emerge with a Gaudí influence: the old Post Office from 1910 in the Catedral square, and the building from 1926 located in the Santo Domingo square on the corner of Ramón y Cajal street and Padre Isla street.

The vigorous urbanistic dynamism of modern Leon is in total contrast with the intimate feeling in the old city, which has recuperated all its splendour for the stroller after the pedestrianisation of many of the most emblematic artistic areas. Furthermore, the San Marcos square where we can find the *Parador Nacional* (National Inn) has been remodelled, the traffic has been cut on the bridge over Bernesga and it has been given back to the passers-by and pilgrims who used to use this road when leaving Leon on the way to Compostela.

The older districts, Santa Marina, San Martín, Santa Ana, and El Mercado are still very suggestive. The only remaining gate in the city wall, called the Puerta Castillo, is to be found in the Santa Marina district, and very close to the church we find the Corral of San Guisán, the spot where the patriotic rising

against the French took place. Some small squares like the Vizconde square and the San Pelayo square complete the unique physiognomy of this district. The latter, which is to be found secluded in the patio of a college, is located in what is possibly the oldest civil building of the city: the possible remains of the palace which belonged to Alfonso VII.

The San Martín district is one of the oldest districts outside the Roman walls. Many of its street names bring to mind the occupations of its original inhabitants: *Platerías* (Silversmith), *Carnicerías* (Butchers), *Zapaterías* (Cobblers), *Azabachería* (Mineralogy), *Varillas* (Basket making), and *Ollería* (Pot making). Other names evoke old legends and stories like *Matasiete*, which was the setting for a bloody fight between two

San Martín Square in the «Barrio Húmedo».

Cid Park.

Ancha Street.

Neptuno fountain in the San Francisco Park.

Virgen del Camino Sanctuary: close-up of Saint James and of the Visitation.

noble families, the Castros and the Laras, for motives of love; Santa Cruz street which was renamed after the Jews and the Moors lived there, or the street called Judío Mulhacin, named after a character from the times of Alfonso XI. There is an abundance of taverns and inns in this district, and it is popularly known as the «*Barrio Húmedo*» (Humid District).

The Mercado district is singular for the fact that it shows one of the most typical aspects of rural Leon: the Grano square, or the Mercado square which is still paved in stone with its back to the church, and its fountain, cross, trees, convent, and the crooked streets which surround it.

And finally, there is the Santa Ana district. This is the district which has suffered the most from modern constructions and harassment, although it still does conserve some very attractive corners.

VIRGEN DEL CAMINO SANCTUARY

Six kilometres from the capital on the main road leading to Astorga we can find the image of the Leonese Patroness. The actual building is a modern construction which was designed by brother Coello of Portugal. It was erected in order to substitute the sanctuary built in the 16th century and demolished around the middle of the 20th century. The baroque reredos comes from the old church and is the work of Antonio and Pedro de Valladolid in 1730, and it includes a niche which contains an image of the Virgin of the Road from the 16th century. The stained glass windows were designed by Rafols and made in the Chartres workshop. And finally, the crucifix located in the interior of the temple, as well as the portico sculptures and the sanctuary doors are all first-quality and all work of Subirachs.

Pennants and decorated floats in the Saint Froilán festival.

«Papones» in the Easter Week processions.

LEONESE TRADITIONS

The main Leonese festival takes place during the first half of June in honour of Saint John and Saint Peter. Many folkloric exhibitions, bowling competitions, Leonese fighting competitions, fireworks displays and other events take place. The majority of the cultural evenings take place during the week dedicated to Saint Marcelo, although the Saint Froilán festival celebrated on October 5th displays a more pilgrim side, as it is customary to walk up to the Virgen del Camino sanctuary, and many people from neighbouring regions also take part in this festival.

Easter Week in Leon has been declared to be of National Touristic Interest and it has experienced an unwonted boom in recent years. From Good Friday until Resurrection Sunday many brotherhoods parade through the city with their various «floats» normally carried on the shoulders of «papones» (ghost-like figures). One of the oldest and most attractive processions takes place on Good Friday, when, from 7.30am to 4pm twelve floats and almost four thousand brotherhoods file past.

On the last Sunday in April the Cabezadas ceremony takes place opposite the Saint Isidore basilica, and on the first Sunday in October a similar ceremony takes place in the cloister of the cathedral. It is known as the Foro u Oferta (Forum and Offering) and is an age-old thanks-giving by the Leonese City Council for the victory won in the battle of Clavijo.

And an ingrained tradition in the city is the customary alternating in the Húmedo district, the authentic paradise of *tapas*, wine, and good atmosphere. In the heart of the San Martín district there is an unusually high concentration of bars, pubs, taverns, and inns on the many streets which begin and end at the Tiendas square, and there is a constant hubbub of people entering and leaving, sampling the appetisers in the afternoon and on a constant and lively «pub crawl» in the evening and on into the night.

During Easter Week there is also the custom, which has become popular in practically all the bars of the capital, called «killing Jews». It consists of drinking a lemonade made from wine, lemons, spices, and whatever else an imaginative mind may wish to add.

Ceremony of the Prolonged Singing in the cloister of the Cathedral.

Astorga from the San Justo de la Vega road.

THE PROVINCE

ARBAS

The Collegiate Church of Santa María de Arbas is located just a short distance from the border between Asturias and Leon in the heart of the Pajares pass. It is very possible that the present building comes from the era of Alfonso IX, and was used as a place of rest for the pilgrims after their difficult and tiring walk to the pass. The church consists of three naves with their corresponding chapels in the upper part. The lateral apses are square while the central apse is distinguished for its moulded ornamentation in the vault similar to that used in the dome of the cathedral in Zamorra. The excellent capitals and the

decoration of the building is extremely interesting. The restoration undertaken a few years ago is considered to be one of the best in the whole province.

ALIJA DEL INFANTADO

Close to La Bañeza, in Alija del Infantado which is located beside the bordering line between Leon and Zamorra, one can find the ruins of a castle from the 15th century which was owned by the Ponce family; it is currently the property of the Duke of Infantado. The building is a square construction with round turrets at the corners and small towers in the centre of the walls. On the inside of the castle grounds there is an old building from the 13th century.

Close to Alija, in the San Esteban de Nogales locality lie the remains of the old Cistercian monastery with its broad cultural tradition since its foundation in the 13th century. One can also visit Quintana del Marco with its abundant and excellent Roman remains stored in the National Archaeology Museum and in the Leon Museum. A special mention must be given to the bust by Marco Aurelio which is located in the upper part of the parish church and is popularly known as «Saint Peter».

ASTORGA

Episcopal headquarters, capital of Maragatería, and one of the most important cities founded by the Romans and baptised *Astúrica Augusta*. Astorga is a city which has a rich monumental history. Of great importance are the Roman structures which have appeared during the course of various excavations and constructions, although the walls have only been preserved in part after being restored in the Middle Ages; the Ergástula is also from the same era, an area which served as a prison until recent times.

Construction began on the Santa María Cathedral in 1471 on the same site as the old temple from the 11th century, but work was not finished until the 18th century. In the complex architecture of the Leonese cathedral various different styles are evident: flamboyant gothic, renaissance and baroque. There are

Astorga: Walls, Episcopal Palace and Cathedral.

Carracedo Monastery.

outstanding articles inside: the main reredos, a majestic work by Gaspar Becerra, consists of three bodies adapted to the apse, and it displays a beautiful image of the Virgin known as «Her Majesty» from the Roman era with Byzantine influences; the splendid walnut pulpit adorned with artistic bas-reliefs; the choir seating, an exceptional work from the 16th century; the superb doors displaying elegant reliefs and an Immaculate by Gregorio Fernández.

The Episcopal Palace was built by Antonio Gaudi at the request of the bishop of Astorga, the Catalan monsignor Grau Vallespinós, and like the brilliant architect, a native of Reus. At present, it is home to the Caminos Museum and contains some wonderful collections of Romanesque sculptures, gold and silver pieces, paintings, and a very select collection of Roman and medieval epigraphs.

BOÑAR

The small town of Boñar is set on the banks of the Porma river, a par excellence summer town with beautiful surroundings. Quite close by, towards the north, the Porma reservoir is set amid valleys and peaks with spectacular views and the possibility of practising aquatic sports.

CARRACEDO

Between Ponferrada and Cacabelos, the old monastery of Carracedo is set in a town of the same name. It was founded in 990 by Bermudo II although a short time later it was totally demolished by the Arabs. Having been reconstructed at the beginning of the 12th century by Alfonso VII it came to rest with the Cistercian order. Subsequently, Alfonso IX built an independent castle, but later restorations caused various sections to lose their Romanesque architecture. The monastery was abandoned after the Deamortisation and it suffered grave deterioration. A restoration campaign undertaken a few years ago succeeded in giving back the dignity lost in these venerable stones. The Chapter house with its gothic vaults from the 12th century has been preserved, as has a part of the cloister, the refectory, and various other rooms from the 16th century. In the palace, one must visit the «kitchen of the queen» and the bay windows, the vestibule with the estimable relief of her Majesty, and a beautiful gallery with pointed arches.

The parish church of Carracedo still conserves some architectural traces from the 12th century, and it was reconstructed towards the end of the 18th century.

CARRIZO DE LA RIBERA

On the banks of the Orbigo stands the Santa María de Carrizo monastery run by the Cistercian monks. It was founded by *doña* Estefanía Ramírez, the widow of the Count Ponce de Minerva who erected the monastery in Sandoval. Its construction dates back to the 12th century, and the three semicircular apses, as well as the doorway on the north are also from this era. The main chapel, restored in the 17th century, is covered with vaulted plasterwork, although the major part of the building is from the 18th century. The reredos is baroque (1676) with sculptures by José Mayo.

Two aspects of the Carracedo Monastery.

Doorway and interior of the Santa María de Carrizo Monastery.

CASTRILLO DE LOS POLVAZARES

Having been miraculously preserved through the passage of time, Castrillo de los Polvazares, which is located just a few kilometres from Astorga on the Jacobea Route, is architecturally the ideal prototype of a Leonese town. Ochre stone houses, large green doorways big enough to let the carriages through, and the stone paving on the streets – and all this in perfect condition. This is why it has been declared a National Monument.

CISTIERNA

Lovely town, very popular in summer, joint capital of high Esla with Riaño. In both there are shopping markets, the most popular products in Cistierna being the «Lazos de San Guillermo» and the typical cured meats.

COMPLUDO

From the locality of El Acebo, whose Jacobin route leads the wanderer through wooden balconied houses, one can reach the road to Compludo. From the old monastery founded by Saint Fructuosus in the 7th century only the two capitals, from this same era, have been preserved in the church. An undoubted tourist attraction is the famous blacksmiths, still in use and which functions with medieval techniques using motive water power. Returning back once again to the Road to Santiago one reaches Riego de Am-

Castrillo de los Polvazares.

Panoramic view of Cistierna.

Blacksmiths in Compludo.

bros and Molinaseca where one can admire the Nuestra Señora de las Angustias Sanctuary (Our Lady of Mercy) and stroll through the charming side-streets after sampling the typical cured meats of the area.

CORULLON

This locality enjoys some beautifully panoramic views, and especially from the area by the castle, which was built towards the end of the 14th century and owned by the marquis of Villafranca. The two Romanesque churches which have been conserved are of great artistic value. The San Esteban church displays a beautiful doorway, and the San Miguel

Castle in Corullón.

church from the end of the 12th century is distinguished for its sculptural ornamentation, and the corbels on the eaves are extremely interesting.

FONCEBADON

In the 12th century King Ramiro II summoned a council in this place, which in olden times was known as Monte Irago. Its altitude (1,490m.) and the absence of inhabitants in the immediate surroundings make this one of the most desolate and amazing stretches in the whole Road to Santiago. In the 12th century there were two hospitals, two churches and a lodgings for pilgrims here, although today the village is abandoned and demolished, and it paints a ghostly picture. A little distance away, on the top of the Foncebadón pass, the dividing line between Maragatería and Bierzo, one will find the Ferro Cross with its base covered in stones which passing pilgrims have left there down through the centuries. Going towards the Bierzo region there are many uninhabited villages, as is the case of Manjarín and Labor del Rey only two kilometres to the southwest with their always amazing scenery.

GRADEFES

This village is located on the banks of the river Esla, just 34 kilometres from the capital of the province.

Apse of the Cistercian Monastery in Gradefes.

Partial view of Grajal de Campos.

It is home to the Santa María la Real monastery which is run by Cistercian nuns, and its construction began in 12th century. The predominant style in the construction of this building is Romanesque, and from this era it conserves the upper end, the nave around the apse, and the transept as the most representative pieces from the original building. Work in this monastery continued through the 13th and 14th centuries, and it was finally finished with the construction of the choir at the foot of the church in the 15th century. It has the curious characteristic of being the only church in Spain run by the feminine sector of the Cistercian order which has a nave around the apse.

In its interior, the monastery guards the sepulchres of its founders, an extraordinary carving of the Virgin and Child from the 13th century, and various other artistic pieces in the monastery's museum.

GRAJAL DE CAMPOS

In the heart of the Tierra de Campos we can find the best conserved castle of the whole Leonese province. The Grajal fortress is from the beginning of the 16th century and it is imminently a defensive structure. It has a vast square structure with round turrets in the corners, many small windows for the artillery pieces, and amazingly solid walls finished off with battlements.

The palace belonging to the marquis of Grajal is from the same time, and its construction was modelled on the palace belonging to the archbishop of Alcalá de Henares. What stands out is the sober façade with its two towers, the patio with a double gallery and the arcades with four and five half-pointed arches, and a beautiful staircase.

La Bañeza: Astorga Street.

The San Miguel church was built between the 16th and 17th centuries. It consists of three naves with arches supported on Tuscan columns, and a plasterwork vault. The Christ and the Nazarene by Pedro de la Cuadra are also worth mentioning.

LA BAÑEZA

Asturians and Romans established their dominions here. The medieval era left its mark on the San Salvador church, rebuilt in the 11th and 12th centuries after being destroyed by Almanzor. For its part,

La Bañeza: Main Square.

Gorges of Valdeteja in the Curueño river.

the Santa María church displays a transept from the 16th century, three naves from the 17th century, and an unfinished tower from the 18th century. The main reredos is from the 17th century, and a carving of the Dolores (the Grievous) by Gregorio Fernández.

LA VECILLA

The Curueño, a par excellence trout river, rises in the spurs of the Vegarada pass, and after leaving behind valleys and beautiful picturesque villages it flows almost parallel to a Roman road and the limestone undermining of Valdeteja, and the gorges which bears its name. On leaving the mountainous massif it flows around La Vecilla, a town with a medieval history, conserving a turret from this era, and also a town with a great summer tradition.

LANCIA (VILLASABARIEGO)

On the upper part of the hillocks visible on the left from the road which leads from Puente Villarente to Mansilla there is an archaeological deposit which contains the remains of Lancia, the most important city in Asturias. It was destroyed by the legions of the Roman general Tito Carisio, and was subsequently inhabited by the Romans. From this era remains have been found of a market, various streets and a part of the hot springs, together with some important materials deposited in the Museum of Leon.

LAS MEDULAS

They were declared Heritage of Humanity in 1998. They are located 25 kilometres from Ponferrada taking the main road towards Vigo and with a turnoff to the left in the town of Carucedo. The best views can be enjoyed from the Orellán vantage point, although one can also traverse the lower areas. The Las Medulas are what remains of the gold mining work done by the Romans from the first century of the Christian era, and whose custody and administration was what motivated the military contingent in the northwest of Spain. The system used in mining the gold consisted of making holes in the upper part of the bed with the galleries and shafts, injecting water already stored in dams at great pressure, and in this way provoking collapse, and later filtering and cleaning the deposits of earth using large washing machines. It has been calculated that no less than 40 thousand slaves, the majority being Asturians and Celts, worked during two centuries in these mines, and the loss of life was very elevated. The other fundamental aspect was the water, channelled through canals designed with admirable precision, which came from the rivers and streams in the

Teleno and Cabrera mountains, and especially from the Cabo river located 28 Km away as the crow flies. What can be seen today are the remains of that colossal mining work which moved approximately three hundred million tons of earth.

The Carucedo lake located close to Las Medulas is an artificial lake, having been provoked by the water deposited after filtering and washing the earth.

LOS ANCARES

Under the generic name of Los Ancares coming from the mountain range of more that thirty kilometres in length which serves as a border between three provinces. Los Ancares takes in an area which comprises of the southeast part of the Lugo province, the southwest of the Principality of Asturias, and the northwest of Leon. To be exact, the Leonese Ancares extends over an area which measures 530 square kilometres, and includes some very important villages and towns like Candín, Tejedo de Ancares, Balouta, Campo del Agua, Villar de Acero, and Porcarizas.

The singular geography of this spot which has kept it far from the large and important roadways, the climate, and the difficulty in cultivating the land has contributed to its isolation from external influences

Dawn in Las Médulas.

Oseja de Sajambre, in the Peaks of Europe.

on a human and ecological level. In Las Ancares one can still find one of the oldest constructions in Europe, the *Palloza,* whose similarity to the Celtic cabins is notable, although with certain adaptations in tune with the geography of this area. Some of these cabins can be seen in Balouta and Campo del Agua, or in Piornedo in the province of Lugo after passing by the Ancares Pass at an altitude of 1,670 metres.

THE PEAKS OF EUROPE

They serve as a natural border between the north-east of Leon, the Asturian Principality, and the Cantabrian community. This is a mountainous area situated in the central part of the Cantabria range, culminating in the Torre Cerredo (2,648m.), and with depressions as deep as that of Cain where the Garganta del Cares begins with its 11Km crossing through an impressive gorge. The Santa Marina and Posada de Valdeón villages offer incredibly beautiful scenes of cliffs and craggy rocks, and luscious forests of beach trees during the descent from the Pandetrave pass. The Tombo vantage point close to the Cordiñanes is especially recommended for its picturesque view. From here one can reach the hermitage of Corona, a heavenly spot, and the «*chorco de los lobos*» (trap of the wolves), an ancestral trap for catching these animals.

A street in Mansilla de las Mulas.

MANSILLA DE LAS MULAS

An undoubted medieval village which even today conserves traces typical of this era. The walls are a National Monument and they totally surround the urban nucleus. They were built by Fernando II around 1181 after repopulating the town. These walls consist of a solid construction of lime and pebbles, and finished off with battlements devoid of loopholes, together with towers, six being semi-cylindrical, and of which some still stand today. Before reaching the walls one must go through a gateway under which there is a passage with a pointed vault. The Mansilla walls are considered to be the most important medieval fortress of the province.

Walls in Mansilla de las Mulas.

General view of the San Pedro de Montes Monastery.

MONTES DE VALDUEZA

Hardly a trace remains of the San Pedro de Montes monastery founded by Saint Fructuosus in the 7th century; the only remains are epigraphs, a cross, and a decorated storm door over the Santa Cruz hermitage on the outskirts of the town. The installations of the monastery underwent important reformations from the 9th and 10th centuries until the neoclassic and baroque eras. A fire occurring around the middle of the 19th century left the place in ruins. In the church's interior there still remains Romanesque carvings and some remains of the seating used by the monks.

Close-up of a capital.

The church interior. ▷

Partial view of Peñalba de Santiago.

NAVATEJERA

The town of Navatejera is to be found a little more than three kilometres from Leon on the banks of the river Torío. Here, in 1885 a Roman village was discovered with three bodies of buildings. The noble area, or the Master's residence dates back to the 4th century of the Christian era, and the hot springs area is from earlier times considering the type of ceramics found. Three of the residential halls, one of which has an octagonal shape, display some exquisite mosaics. There are indications that some of the buildings were used for religious purposes, or to be more precise, for purposes of the Christian religion.

PEÑALBA DE SANTIAGO

A locality situated in an idyllic spot in the Valle de Silencio, and with different and interesting traces of rural architecture.
Peñalba is sheltered by a whitish calcareous cliff, from here its name, where the abbot Solomon built a Mozarabic monastery in 937.
The church has just one nave with an apse on either side, and it displays a beautiful doorway which has two very elegant horseshoe arches making this monument, together with the San Miguel de Escalada, some of the best work in the Leonese Mozarabic architecture.

Mozarabic church.

A street with balconies and the doorway of the Mozarabic church.

Templar's Castle in Ponferrada.

PONFERRADA

An important industrial and mining town of Roman origin which takes its name from the iron railings built by bishop Osmundo of Astorga in the 11th century for the transit of pilgrims of the Road to Santiago. Ponferrada reckons with a great monumental richness. The Templar's castle was built in the 12th century and was the residence of the Commander of this Order, although it underwent changes in the 15th century when it became the property of the Catholic Kings. The Encina Basilica from the 16th century worships the patroness of the Bierzo. The Santa María of

Encina Basilica.

Chapel in the Santo Tomás de las Ollas Church.

Riaño from the other side of the reservoir.

Vizbayo church is from the 11th century, and the San Andrés church dates back to the 13th century.

Very close to Ponferrada we can find the Santo Tomás de las Ollas church, a Mozarabic church which was built in the 10th century and belonged to the San Pedro de Montes monastery. The chapel at the upper end has a horseshoe arch over the entrance, and a blind arcade presenting nine arches, also horseshoe arches. It seems that the name «Ollas» (pots or pans) comes from the factory in the monastery which made vessels and containers.

RIAÑO

A double access route to the region of Valdeón, in the Peaks of Europe, and in the Sajambre region by the Pontón pass, as well as new location for one of the most beautiful towns which belonged to Leon, a town whose ruins is to be found hidden at the bottom of the reservoir.

The new Riaño, built on the banks of the colossal mass of water dammed by the Esla since 1990, has forgotten its cattle-raising past and has put its bets on tourism and all things modern. It conserves the main door of a travelling church which originally belonged to Siero de la Reina but was moved to Pedrosa de Rey, dismantled, and permanently set up in this spot.

From Riaño one can go on various mountain excursions in the surrounding areas. And without forgetting the adjoining villages which were saved from drowning like Boca de Huérgano, Burón, or the area taken in by what is called Land of the Queen.

San Tirso Church, Sahagún.

SAHAGUN

Its historical and artistic tradition is due to the fact that it is an important stretch in the Road to Santiago, and a place favoured by Alfonso VI, who extended its monastic centre. This same king, as well as three of his wives are buried in the church of the present San Benito monastery which is temporarily held by the Benedictine nuns. It conserves very little of its original magnificence due to the fires suffered and the fact that it was abandoned in the 19th century after the Deamortisation. Remains of the apse can still be seen, as can a part of the transept and the neoclassic doorway. In the monastery's museum there are many interesting pieces, among which we can find a wonderful monstrance by Enrique de Arfe.

Other interesting monuments include the Santo Tirso church from the 12th century, a Mudejar church in brick, and the San Lorenzo church, from the early 17th century, similar to the former although with a gothic influence and a varied artistic heritage in its interior.

And finally, the Peregrina Sanctuary from the 13th century, also in brick, and with exquisite Mauresque plasterwork in the chapel belonging to the Castros family.

A few kilometres from Sahagun we come across the ruins of the old Trianos monastery, and the splendid ecclesiastic San Pedro de Dueñas monastery run by the Benedictine nuns, a Romanesque building in brick with beautiful capitals and an amazing life-size Christ by Gregorio Fernández.

San Miguel de Escalada Church.

SAN MIGUEL DE ESCALADA

One of the most interesting churches from the so-called Mozarabic or re-population art. It was built in 913 by a group of monks from Cordova who were fleeing from Muslim persecutions. The church displays a rich decoration on the storm doors and tympanums, and with horseshoe arches which have been taken from other older buildings, especially those which have been used in the capitals, being mostly Roman and Visigoth. The interior has a basilical ground plan with an «iconostasis» of Oriental origin which separates the sacred area from the public seating area. The portico, which was built after the church, consists of twelve horseshoe arches, while

Interior of San Miguel de Escalda Church.

Castle in Valencia de Don Juan.

Vegacervera gorges. ▷

the tower, quite jagged after many restorations, forms a part of a Romanesque body by the name of Panteón de Abades which is from the 11th century. The Villarmún locality is just a few kilometres from Escalada, and it has a church which belongs to the transition period between Mozarabic and Roman architecture, and it has traces of both of these styles, especially in the triumphal arch in the shape of a horseshoe.

VALENCIA DE DON JUAN

In the old Coyanza area, celebrated for the fact that it acted as the headquarters for the Council convoked by Fernando I in 1048. Its castle was taken by Almanzor in 996 and later by Alfonso VIII de Castilla. The present state of its remains from the 15th century, with

its spectacular tower, has awarded it the honour of being one of the most important military fortresses in the province. The Nuestra Señora del Castillo Viejo church guards an image from the 12th century, patroness of the town, as well as an excellent Descent in the Becerra school. The San Pedro Herrerian style parish church shelters a monumental reredos from the 16th century, work of Guillermo Doncel.

VEGACERVERA

One of the most beautiful enclaves of the whole province, and situated at the entrance to one of the spectacular gorges excavated by the Torío river during the course of thousands of years. The town conserves some houses which have coats of arms on

Valporquero Caves.

their walls, and as well as the scenery it also offers some wonderful cured meats which can be enjoyed in the open mountain air. In November, this town celebrates a fair dedicated to the sampling and worshipping of cured goat's meat.

Past Hoces de Vegacevera in a village called Felmín one can reach the road which leads up to the Valporquero Caves, one of the most amazing geological jewels in Spain.

VILLAFRANCA DEL BIERZO

The lands of the Bierzo provide the visitor with some spectacular views, among which the vineyards and the horticultural crops stand out. Its old capital of Roman origin, Cacabelos, is a sanctuary of wine.

Furthermore it displays its Celtic, Asturian, and Roman traces in the very interesting Archaeology Museum, and without forgetting the Nuestra Señora de la Quinta Angustia church, and the Santa María church from the 16th century.

Villafranca is the capital of the Bierzo region. It has an ancestry which is centuries old, and it has a very attractive urban structure with crooked streets flanked by stately homes and palaces. Every corner of Villafranca offers the feeling of an old city with an illustrious historical past, and especially in Agua street where stately mansions alternate with hidden taverns perfect for sampling the great wine of the Bierzo region. Among its interesting monuments we should mention the Marquis of Villafranca Castle, presently the property of the counts of Peña Ramiro; the San Francisco convent with its Romanesque entrance and

Agua Street.

nave with Mauresque ceilings decorated with Mudejar paintings and coats of arms, as well as the seating from the 16th century, and the baroque reredos; the Santa María Collegiate church from the 16th century designed by Rodrigo Gil de Hontañón, and the Anunciada convent with its Renaissance doorway, which hoards a reredos from the Gaspar Becerra school, the Saint Lorenzo of Brindisi sepulchre, and the pantheon of the Alvarez family from Toledo. And finally, the Romanesque Santiago church with its single nave, and which stands out because of its north doorway with eight exquisite capitals, and its crucified Christ of great expressiveness from the 14th century.

The Santa María Collegiate church

Doorways and close-up of the Santa María de Sandoval Monastery.

VILLAVERDE DE SANDOVAL

Close to this town and not far from the Road to Santiago we can find the ruins of the Cistercian Santa María de Sandoval monastery. It was founded in 1176 by the servant of King Alfonso VII, the count Ponce de Minerva and his wife whose sepulchres are conserved in the main altar of the church. The construction is from the 12th century, and it has three naves with their corresponding apses in the typical Cistercian style. The cloister is from the 17th century. Inside the church there is a beautiful poly-chromed wooden relief from the 16th century which depicts a dead Christ accompanied by His Mother and other characters. Also very impressive is the monumental Mozarabic capital used as a holy-water stoup.

FESTIVALS AND POPULAR TRADITIONS

When making a list of the popular festivals and traditions which take place all through the year, the first we must mention is the *Carnavales* which has an influence in many towns, and especially in La Bañeza. During three days La Bañeza undergoes a total transformation and the town is lavished with colour, happiness, feasts and masks, each one more imaginative than the next, welcoming the thousands of visitors who come from near and far every year in order to participate in, and witness this spectacle. Another festival celebrated in Astorga is the «*Piñata*

Saturday», after Ash Wednesday, and it consists of a colourful and attractive procession of groups of masked Bañezans.

Easter Week, as well as in Leon, has four interesting locations: Ponferrada, Villafranca del Bierzo, Astorga, and La Bañeza. The respective brotherhoods swarm the streets with estimable statues in the middle of a grand retreat. Some of the processions are celebrated at night, as is the case in Astorga and Villafranca, and this contributes to even more sensationalism.

The Corpus Christi festival has special significance in Laguna de Negrillos where a dance procession (only the men dance with white petticoats) of figure-

Old carnival in Velilla de la Reina.

Easter Week processions.

Leonese fighting ring.

heads covered with masks and other elements grant this grand event a distinction of its own.

During the month of June the Poetry Festival takes place in Villafranca del Bierzo which takes in the National Competition and the Poets of Bierzo Meeting. Apart from the popular pilgrimages dedicated to the Virgin, which populate the Leonese localities (Castrotierra, Camposagrado, Carrasconte, La Velilla, etc.) there are other popular events with the typical products of the area being the protagonists –the Garlic festival in Santa Marina del Rey, the exaltation of the *Botillo* (large stuffed pork sausage) in the Bierzo, the Pepper festival in Fresno de la Vega, or the Leek fair in Sahagún–. The Shepherd's festival celebrated in Barrios de Luna is above all a

Bowls competition.

«Leonese mastiff» competition, a dog very much used in the shepherd's work. On August 15th there is a Horse festival celebrated in Maraña, close to Riaño, with horses galloping bareback in various races. And finally there is the Leonese fighting, of Asturian origin, which takes place in the «fighting rings» in Curueño, Cisterna, La Vecilla, and Leon.

One of the most traditional suits worn in the province is called the *maragato*, and it is worn in many of the festivals of the region, especially in Astorga and Santa Colomba de Somoza, and even more so in Castrillo de los Polvazares, a locality where the colourful and traditional *maragata* weddings are celebrated.

CUISINE

In Leon and in the surrounding province there are some delicious plates, some of which have originally come from other parts of Spain but have been given that special Leonese touch. The «*botillo*» has succeeded in becoming a very popular dish through the width and breadth of Spain. Pork ribs and tail, and various cured meats seasoned with salt, pepper and garlic, and all wrapped in the pig's intestines is the base of this unique dish ideal for supporting any type of adverse climate.

Offal in the shape of tripe, sweetbreads, kidneys, blood, etc. are basic ingredients for some of the exquisite *tapas* which can be sampled at any time in any part of the province.

The «*cocido maragato*» (a type of stew) has the peculiarity of being eaten the wrong way around, leaving the soup until last, and the «*calderetas de cordero*» (lamb stew) is excellently prepared in many of the mountain bars.

The pure and cold mountain air is perfect for preparing *chorizo*, *lomo*, and *cecina* (all cured meats) and for giving them an unbeatable taste, while the rivers provide trout which is always a reference in this exquisite and varied cuisine. The frog's legs in *La Bañeza* and the cod in *Valderas* are also very tasty dishes. Mansilla and Sahagún always attract the lovers of good food.

Leonese meats.

The excellent wines of the province have begun to take root in this very difficult market. The most famous wines of the Bierzo region, reds whites and rosés , are truly exquisite, and little by little the wines of Valdevimbre and Los Oteros are consolidating their prestige. In Gordoncillo we can even say that they are living new experiences as the innovative «Gordoncello» company, with its own vineyards and modern technology, has begun to bottle first quality wine with an exceptional bouquet in 1999.

And finally, the list of sweets and desserts is multiplying in every Leonese locality. The *Mantecadas* in Astorga, Almond *Amarguillos* from Sahagún, *Imperials* from La Bañeza, *Lazos* from San Guillermo en Cisterna, and the *Nicanores* from Boñar have all crossed the provincial frontiers due to their quality and well-deserved prestige.

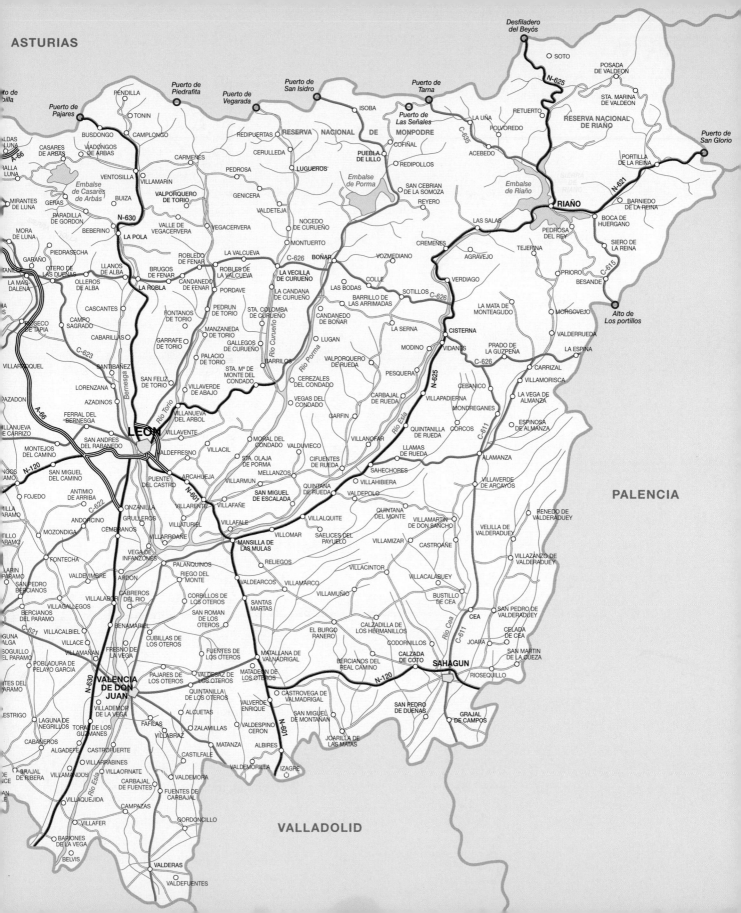

CONTENTS

EDITORIAL ESCUDO DE ORO, S.A.
I.S.B.N. 84-378-2154-1
Printed by FISA - Escudo de Oro, S.A.
Legal Dep. B. 23772-2005

Protegemos el bosque; papel procedente de cultivos forestales controlados
Wir schützen den Wald. Papier aus kontrollierten Forsten.
We protect our forests. The paper used comes from controlled forestry plantations
Nous sauvegardons la forêt: papier provenant de cultures forestières contrôlées